W A I T
for D A D D Y 's
H U G

Written and Illustrated

by Rochelle Cunningham

A Domestic Wildflower Book

ISBN-13: 978-1500558680 (pbk)

ISBN-10: 1500558680

A Domestic Wildflower Book

Published by Domestic Wildflower Press, LLC

Boise, ID 83704

Design: R. Cunningham

Printed and bound in United States

Dedicated to

CHILDREN

With parents working in

THE OIL FIELDS

And to Kelly ~

for manifesting more than Buffalo's with me

in the Badlands of North Dakota.

One more hug before Daddy has to leave for work.

He won't be home for dinner tonight, or even tomorrow night.

It will be sixteen nights,

until they see him again,

and get another hug.

So Daddy makes it a GOOD one!

While Daddy drives many miles into the night –

Mommy tucks her little ones into bed.

She dries their tears from missing Daddy.

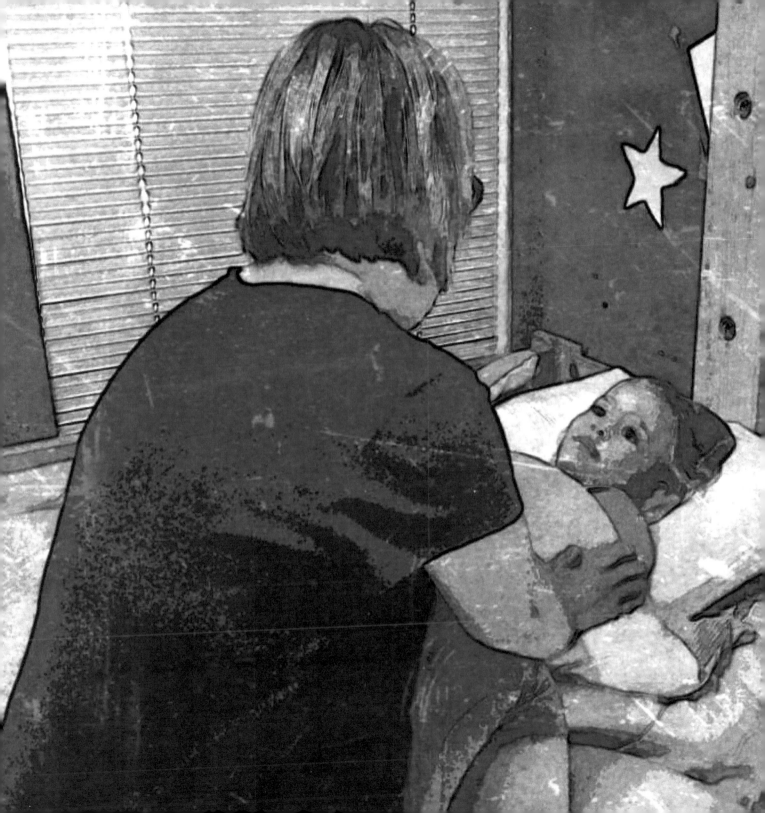

When Daddy arrives at work,

he calls to let everyone know he is safe.

Then he must get some sleep after such a long drive.
He has to get up early the next morning,
to start his long job.

Daddy's first day of work,

is the beginning of his fourteen day 'hitch'.

The first few days of every 'hitch' in the oil field are the hardest.

Everyone is sad to be apart,

but they all know that Daddy will be back home

in FIFTEEN days!

Everyone goes on with their lives.

While Daddies work hard out in the oil fields –

    Mommies work hard taking care of the kids at home.

And everyone counts down the days –

    until they are all together again.

Talking on the phone is how everybody stays close to Daddy.

This is the good part –

hearing his voice!

Sometimes it's hard to go to bed,
without telling him one more time -

"I love you, Dad."

Even though Daddy is far away working at his busy job,
    everyone talks
        every single day.

Sometimes they talk about school,
    sometimes they talk about who has a boo-boo,
        sometimes they talk about who is helping mommy,

And sometimes –

They talk about all the fun times they will have,

just as soon,

as Daddy returns.

Life is about counting the days,

   until Daddy comes home.

Everyone looks forward to seeing Daddy on his days off –

   and they HOPE to be together,

      for ALL the special moments.

No matter what Daddy is doing,

    he is always thinking of his family back home.

"Hi Daddy! What are you doing?"

    "I'm missing you!"

"Really? You are? You're missing me right now?"

    "Yes! I'm missing you bunches and bunches."

"Truckloads and truckloads, Daddy?"

    "Oh, more than that!"

"How much more?"

    "More than anybody can measure, buddy."

Sometimes making plans with Daddy,

    can make the time go by faster.

"Hi, Daddy."

    "Hi, Princess. Did you get the tackle box ready?"

"I sure did! Only nine more days, Daddy!"

    "Only nine more days, baby girl."

Sometimes Daddies get sad,

    when they miss out on things back at home.

But!

    Daddy gets to see pictures of his family –

        on his cell phone and computer.

And!

    The best part is –

        when Daddy comes home,

            they get him for a WHOLE week!

Working in an oil field means that Daddy works

most of the time,

and sleeps the rest of the time.

He lives in a small house with other Daddies,

with a small kitchen,

and a small bathroom –

And all Daddies have very small bedrooms!

All Daddies work hard at their job.

And one thing is for CERTAIN -

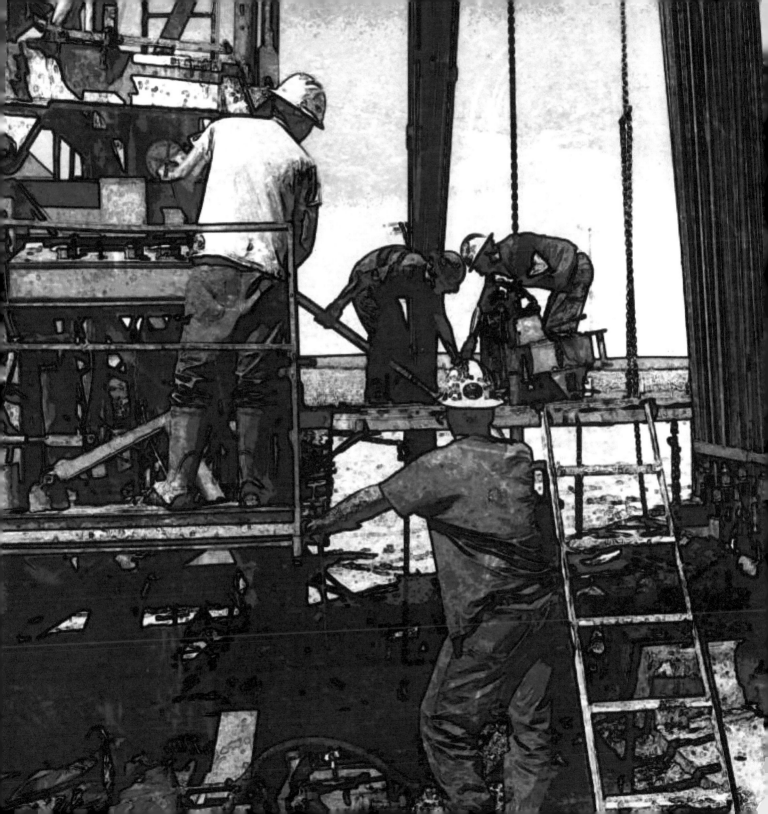

Every single Daddy gets happy when the 'hitch' is almost over!

They look forward to the last day,
            and then,

                        the long drive back home –

Where the excited Mommies,
                and the excited kids,

                        are all waiting –

                                for hugs from Daddy!

But everyone's FAVORITE day –

is day FIFTEEN!

The day,

when Daddy,

is finally home.

ABOUT THE AUTHOR

The author's journey for this story started as curiosity about her brothers occupation and a road trip into the oil fields of North Dakota. It turned into an opportunity to present a heartfelt, tender perspective into a less traditional American lifestyle.

Rochelle Cunningham has earned degrees in Communication, Journalism, and Mediation, and takes great pleasure in writing other people's stories. While in North Dakota, she listened to first hand accounts of life in the oil fields. With encouragement from Kelly "Mama Bear" Brooks (an oil field wife of 16 years), Rochelle decided to create a series of children's books about these men, their careers, and its affect on families.

"Watching these Roughneck Daddies, I realize how helpless my own father must have felt; maintaining that stiff upper lip while his heart broke into a million pieces every time I cried. I clearly remember him on bended knee, many times, holding me until my sobs turned to sniffles, and the sniffles turned to whimpers. I know the pain of good-bye, and the joy of reuniting after a long absence."

Rochelle is honored to give a voice to Oil Field children while having an opportunity to bridge the emotional gap between parent and child.

The next two books in the series will address what kind of work Daddy actually does in the Oil Fields, and a third about how the little ones might better understand Mommies role.

Rochelle J. Cunningham

and Gaius J. Cunningham

June 30, 1942 — January 03, 2011

ACKNOWLEDGEMENTS

To Aspyn and Jarett for their assistance, input, and inspiration.

Many thanks to all my 'little models':

Jason, Tess, Luke, Josh, Nathanial, Madison, Oliver, Eli, and Stella.

To Adam, Kimberly, Debra and Liberty of Watford City.

To the 'grown ups' at the D & A Ranch over Fourth of July.

And to Mickey, Lance, Kim, Ivan, and Kim J. for all the 'hugs'.

Many thanks to my friends, family, and fellow authors for their continued support and encouragement in all my endeavors. Especially to Sherry Briscoe, Troy Lambert, Rodger & Nathan, who all managed to squeeze out precious time to lend me a hand.

To David and Randi for their Sac-enthusiasm and encouragement.

To my readers and critics for all their time, opinions, and suggestions.

And to my brother Sam, for introducing me to North Dakota!

Honorable Mention

Like so many Oil Field family members, I too, am grateful for the dedication, sacrifice, and hard work of all Roughneck workers in North Dakota and beyond. Your wives and children are incredibly generous to share you with America's 'crude' mistress.

CPSIA information can be obtained
at www.ICGtesting.com
Printed in the USA
BVHW020850141218
535626BV00014B/175/P

9 781500 558680